# Ri

# Recipes

# Introduction

Rice is a staple in many countries being served with every meal. It is great resource for bulking up a side dish into a hearty complete meal. Adding countless variety of sauces to rice means that one will never be bored if they chose to have rice every day.

This cookbook is full of ideas to add flavor and pizzazz to any serving of rice. Whether it is with soups, sauces, curries or herbs, this recipe book has something for everyone.

# Perfect White Rice

## Ingredients:

1 cup long grain rice
2 cups water
1 tsp. salt
1 tsp. butter (optional)

## Directions:

1. In a saucepan with a good fitting lid bring water, salt and butter if desired to a boil.
2. Add rice and stir.
3. Cover and reduce heat to medium low.
4. Cook for 20 minutes.
5. Do not lift the lid!
6. The steam that is trapped inside the pan is what allows the rice to cook properly.
7. Remove from heat and fluff with fork.
8. Serve!

# Rice Pilaf

## Ingredients:

2 tbsps. butter
1/2 cup orzo pasta
1/2 cup diced onion
2 cloves garlic, minced
1/2 cup uncooked white rice
2 cups chicken broth

## Directions:

1. Melt the butter in a lidded skillet over medium-low heat.
2. Cook and stir orzo pasta until golden brown.
3. Stir in onion and cook until onion becomes translucent, then add garlic and cook for 1 minute.
4. Mix in the rice and chicken broth. Increase heat to high and bring to a boil.
5. Reduce heat to medium-low, cover, and simmer until the rice is tender, and the liquid has been absorbed, 20 to 25 minutes.
6. Remove from heat and let stand for 5 minutes, then fluff with a fork.

# Spanish Rice

## Ingredients:

1 cup chicken broth
1 cup tomato sauce
6 slices bacon
2 onions, diced
1 cup uncooked white rice
2 tomatoes, diced
2 green bell peppers, diced
1/2 tsp. chili powder
1/2 tsp. salt and ground black pepper
1 (10 oz.) can sliced black olives, drained
1 (10 oz.) can whole kernel corn, drained

## Directions:

1. Bring chicken broth and tomato sauce to a boil in a small saucepan, about 5 minutes.
2. Reduce heat to medium and maintain a simmer while preparing the remaining ingredients.
3. Meanwhile, place bacon in a large skillet and cook over medium-high heat, turning occasionally, until evenly browned, about 10 minutes. Transfer bacon to a paper towel-lined plate, reserving bacon grease in the skillet.
4. Chop bacon.
5. Cook and stir onion in reserved bacon grease over medium heat until tender, about 5 minutes.
6. Stir in rice.
7. Cook and stir until lightly browned, 3 to 5 minutes.
8. Pour boiling chicken broth and tomato sauce into rice mixture.
9. Add tomatoes, green peppers, and chopped bacon.
10. Season with chili powder, salt, and pepper.
11. Cover and simmer until rice is tender and liquid is absorbed, 30 to 40 minutes.
12. Stir black olives and corn into rice mixture before serving.

# Cashew Raisin Rice Pilaf

## Ingredients:

1/4 cup margarine
1 1/2 cups uncooked long grain white rice
1 chopped onion
1 cup chopped carrot
1 cup golden raisins
3 cups chicken broth
3/4 cup uncooked wild rice
2 cups frozen green peas
1 (4 oz.) jar diced pimento peppers, drained
1 cup cashews
1 tsp. salt ground black pepper to taste

## Directions:

1. Melt margarine in a large saucepan over medium-high heat.
2. Sauté the long grain rice, onion, carrot and raisins for 3 to 5 minutes or until onion is tender.
3. Pour in the broth and bring to a boil. Reduce heat to low, cover pan and simmer for 20 to 25 minutes.
4. Meanwhile, in a saucepan bring 1 1/2 cups salted water to a boil.
5. Add wild rice, reduce heat, cover and simmer for 45 minutes.
6. Drain and set aside.
7. When the rice/raisin mixture is finished simmering (rice is cooked), stir in cooked wild rice, peas, pimentos and cashews and heat through.

# Onion Rice Pilaf

## Ingredients:

1/2 small onion, chopped
1 tbsp. butter
1 cup uncooked calrose rice, rinsed
1 1/2 cups chicken broth

## Directions:

1. Heat the butter in a skillet over medium heat.
2. Stir in the onion, and cook until soft and translucent.
3. In a small saucepan, combine the rice, onions, and broth.
4. Bring to a boil over high heat.
5. Reduce heat to low, cover, and simmer 30 minutes. Remove from heat, let cool for several minutes, then fluff with a fork.

# Rice Pilaf with Raisins and Veggies

## Ingredients:

3 cups chicken broth
2 tbsps. olive oil
4 stalks celery, chopped
1/2 large onion, diced
4 green onions, white and green parts separated and sliced
3 cloves garlic, minced
1 tsp. curry powder
1/2 tsp. salt
1 1/2 cups uncooked white rice
1/2 cup golden raisins

## Directions:

1. Bring chicken broth to boil in a saucepan over medium-high heat; continue simmering while preparing remaining ingredients.
2. Heat olive oil in a large skillet over medium heat.
3. Cook and stir celery, onion, green onion white portions, garlic, curry powder, and salt in the hot oil until vegetables are tender, about 5 minutes.
4. Transfer vegetables to a bowl.
5. Cook and stir rice in the same skillet until lightly toasted, about 3 minutes.
6. Stir toasted rice into boiling chicken broth. Reduce heat to medium-low; continue simmering until rice is tender and broth is absorbed, about 15 minutes.
7. Remove rice from heat and stir in raisins, green onion tops, and celery mixture until well blended.

# Mexican Rice

## Ingredients:

1 cup long grain white rice
1 tbsp. vegetable oil
1 1/2 cups chicken broth
1/2 onion, finely chopped
1/2 green bell pepper, finely chopped
1 fresh jalapeno pepper, chopped
1 tomato, seeded and chopped
1 cube chicken bouillon
Salt and pepper to taste
1/2 tsp. ground cumin
1/2 cup chopped fresh cilantro
1 clove garlic, halved

## Directions:

1. In a medium sauce pan, cook rice in oil over medium heat for about 3 minutes.
2. Pour in chicken broth, and bring to a boil.
3. Stir in onion, green pepper, jalapeno, and diced tomato.
4. Season with bouillon cube, salt and pepper, cumin, cilantro, and garlic.
5. Bring to a boil, cover, and reduce heat to low.
6. Cook for 20 minutes.

# Louisiana Red Beans and Rice

## Ingredients:

1 lb. dry kidney beans
1/4 cup olive oil
1 large onion, chopped
1 green bell pepper, chopped
2 tbsps. minced garlic
2 stalks celery, chopped
6 cups water
2 bay leaves
1/2 tsp. cayenne pepper
1 tsp. dried thyme
1/4 tsp. dried sage
1 tbsp. dried parsley
1 tsp. Cajun seasoning
1 pound andouille sausage, sliced
4 cups water
2 cups long grain white rice

## Directions:

1. Rinse beans, and then soak in a large pot of water overnight.
2. In a skillet, heat oil over medium heat. Cook onion, bell pepper, garlic, and celery in olive oil for 3 to 4 minutes.
3. Rinse beans, and transfer to a large pot with 6 cups water.
4. Stir cooked vegetables into beans. Season with bay leaves, cayenne pepper, thyme, sage, parsley, and Cajun seasoning.
5. Bring to a boil, and then reduce heat to medium-low.
6. Simmer for 2 1/2 hours.
7. Stir sausage into beans, and continue to simmer for 30 minutes.
8. Meanwhile, prepare the rice.
9. In a saucepan, bring water and rice to a boil.

10. Reduce heat, cover, and simmer for 20 minutes.
11. Serve beans over steamed white rice.

# Jamaican Rice

## Ingredients:

1 tbsp. vegetable oil
1/2 large onion, sliced
1/2 red apple, cored and sliced
1 pinch curry powder
1 cup water
2/3 cup brown rice
1 tsp. dark molasses or treacle
1 small banana, sliced
1 tbsp. unsweetened flaked coconut

## Directions:

1. Heat the oil in a saucepan over medium heat.
2. Add the onion and red apple.
3. Cook and stir until onion is transparent. Season with curry powder, and stir in the water.
4. Add the rice and molasses, cover, and cook over low heat until the rice is tender, and water has been absorbed, about 30 minutes.
5. Mix in the banana, then sprinkle the coconut on top.
6. Heat through for a moment over low heat before serving.

# Pumpkin Carrot Rice

## Ingredients:

1 1/2 cups brown rice
3 cups water
2 tbsps. olive oil
4 cloves garlic, finely chopped
1 (15 oz.) can pumpkin
2 large carrots, peeled and finely grated
1/4 tsp. salt
1/4 tsp. ground cloves

## Directions:

1. Bring the brown rice and water to a boil in a saucepan over high heat.
2. Reduce heat to medium-low, cover, and simmer until the rice is tender, and the liquid has been absorbed, 45 to 50 minutes.
3. When the rice has nearly finished cooking, heat oil in a large Dutch oven over medium-high heat, and cook and stir garlic just until fragrant.
4. Reduce heat to medium, stir in pumpkin, and cook until heated through, about 1 minute.
5. Stir in carrots and cook for 2 minutes.
6. Stir in salt and cloves.
7. Remove from heat; stir in the cooked rice until well blended. Serve warm.

# Island-Style Fried Rice

## Ingredients:

1 1/2 cups uncooked jasmine rice
3 cups water
2 tsps. canola oil
1 (12 oz.) can luncheon meat, cubed
1/2 cup sliced Chinese pork sausage (lup cheong)
3 eggs, beaten
2 tbsps. canola oil
1 (8 oz.) can pineapple chunks, drained
1/2 cup chopped green onion
3 tbsps. oyster sauce
1/2 tsp. garlic powder

## Directions:

1. Bring the rice and water to a boil in a saucepan over high heat.
2. Reduce heat to medium-low, cover, and simmer until the rice is tender, and the liquid has been absorbed, 20 to 25 minutes.
3. Let the rice cool completely.
4. Heat 2 tsps. of oil in a skillet over medium heat, and brown the luncheon meat and sausage. Set aside, and pour the beaten eggs into the hot skillet.
5. Scramble the eggs, and set aside.
6. Heat 2 tbsps. of oil in a large nonstick skillet over medium heat, and stir in the rice. Toss the rice with the hot oil until heated through and beginning to brown, about 2 minutes.
7. Add the garlic powder, toss the rice for 1 more minute to develop the garlic taste, and stir in the luncheon meat, sausage, scrambled eggs, pineapple, and oyster sauce.
8. Cook and stir until the oyster sauce coats the rice and other ingredients, 2 to 3 minutes, stir in the green onions, and serve.

# Lime Cilantro Rice

## Ingredients:

2 cups water
1 tbsp. butter
1 cup long-grain white rice
1 tsp. lime zest
2 tbsps. fresh lime juice
1/2 cup chopped cilantro

## Directions:

1. Bring the water to a boil; stir the butter and rice into the water.
2. Cover, reduce heat to low, and simmer until the rice is tender, about 20 minutes.
3. Stir the lime zest, lime juice, and cilantro into the cooked rice just before serving.

# Rice Stuffing with Apples, Herbs, and Bacon

## Ingredients:

3 1/2 cups water, divided
1 1/2 cups chicken broth
1 cup uncooked wild rice
1/3 pound bacon
3 cups diced onions
3 cups diced celery
Celery
1 tbsp. water
1 cup uncooked long-grain white rice
1 3/4 cups currants
3/4 cup dried cherries
3/4 cup dried cranberries
1/2 oz. dried apricots
1 cup diced, unpeeled apples
1/2 cup chopped Italian flat leaf parsley
6 tbsps. dried mixed herbs

## Directions:

1. In a medium saucepan over medium heat, bring 1 1/2 cups water and the chicken broth to a boil.
2. Stir in wild rice. Cover, reduce heat, and simmer 45 minutes.
3. Place bacon in a large, deep skillet. Cook over medium high heat until evenly brown. Reserving drippings, drain bacon, crumble, and set aside.
4. In the skillet with the reserved bacon drippings, sauté onions and celery with 1 tbsp. water. Cook until very soft, about 20 minutes.
5. Stir remaining water, white rice, currants, cherries, cranberries, apricots, and apples into the wild rice.
6. Continue cooking 20 minutes, or until wild rice and white rice are tender.

7. In a large bowl, mix the bacon and the onion mixture into the rice mixture.
8. Season with the Italian parsley and dried mixed herbs.

# Mahi Mahi with Coconut Rice and Mango Salsa

## Ingredients:

2 tbsps. olive oil
1 1/2 tsps. soy sauce
2 tsps. lemon juice
1 clove garlic, crushed
2 tsps. red pepper flakes
1 tsp. fresh ground black pepper
1/2 tsp. minced fresh ginger root
2 tbsps. green onion, chopped
Salt to taste
4 (4 oz.) mahi mahi fillets
2 cups uncooked jasmine rice
2 cups water
1 cube chicken bouillon
1 tbsp. butter (optional)
3/4 (14 oz.) can coconut milk
2 tbsps. white sugar
1 1/2 tsps. butter
1 1/2 tbsps. white sugar
1 1/2 cups fresh mango, cubed

## Directions:

1. Whisk together the olive oil, soy sauce, lemon juice, garlic, red pepper flakes, black pepper, ginger, green onion, and salt in a bowl.
2. Add the mahi mahi and toss to evenly coat.
3. Cover the bowl with plastic wrap, and marinate in the refrigerator for 1 hour.
4. Preheat the oven's broiler and set the oven rack in the middle of the oven.
5. Bring the rice, water, chicken bouillon, and 1 tbsp. butter to a boil in a saucepan over high heat.
6. Reduce heat to medium-low, cover, and simmer until the liquid has been absorbed, about 20 minutes.

7. Pour in the coconut milk and 2 tbsps. of sugar.
8. Stir, and simmer uncovered until the rice has absorbed most of the coconut milk.
9. While the rice is cooking, remove the mahi mahi from the marinade, and shake off excess. Discard the remaining marinade.
10. Place fish in a large baking dish in a single layer.
11. Broil in the preheated oven until the fish flakes easily with a fork, 10 to 15 minutes. If the fish browns too quickly, cover the baking dish with a sheet of aluminum foil.
12. Melt 1 1/2 tsps. butter and 1 1/2 tbsps. of sugar in a skillet over medium-high heat.
13. When the mixture begins to bubble, stir in mango cubes.
14. Cook and stir until mango is tender, about 5 minutes.
15. Serve by placing a mahi mahi fillet over a scoop of hot rice and top with the mango salsa.

# Asian Coconut Rice

## Ingredients:

1 (14 oz.) can coconut milk
1 1/4 cups water
1 tsp. sugar
1 pinch salt
1 1/2 cups uncooked jasmine rice

## Directions:

1. In a saucepan, combine coconut milk, water, sugar, and salt.
2. Stir until sugar is dissolved. Stir in rice.
3. Bring to a boil over medium heat.
4. Cover, reduce heat, and simmer 18 to 20 minutes, until rice is tender.

# Paella

### Chicken Ingredients:

1 tbsp. sweet or smoked paprika
2 tsps. oregano
1 (3 lb.) frying chicken, cut into 10 pieces

### Paella Ingredients:

1/4 cup extra-virgin olive oil
2 Spanish chorizo sausages, thickly sliced
Kosher salt and freshly ground pepper
1 Spanish onion, diced
4 garlic cloves, crushed
1 bunch flat-leaf parsley leaves, chopped, reserve some for garnish
1 (15-oz.) can whole tomatoes, drained and hand-crushed
4 cups short grain Spanish rice
6 cups water, warm
Generous pinch saffron threads
1 dozen littleneck clams, scrubbed
1 pound jumbo shrimp, peeled and de-veined
2 lobster tails
1/2 cup sweet peas, frozen and thawed
Lemon wedges, for serving

### Special equipment:

Large paella pan or wide shallow skillet

### Directions:

1. Combine the paprika and oregano in a small bowl.
2. Rub the spice mix all over the chicken and marinate chicken for 1 hour in the refrigerator.
3. Heat oil in a paella pan over medium-high heat.
4. Sauté the chorizo until browned, remove and reserve.
5. Add chicken skin-side down and brown on all sides, turning with tongs.
6. Add salt and freshly ground pepper.
7. Remove from pan and reserve.

8. In the same pan, make a sofrito by sautéing the onions, garlic, and parsley.
9. Cook for 2 or 3 minutes on a medium heat.
10. Then, add tomatoes and cook until the mixture caramelizes a bit and the flavors meld.
11. Fold in the rice and stir-fry to coat the grains.
12. Pour in water and simmer for 10 minutes, gently moving the pan around so the rice cooks evenly and absorbs the liquid.
13. Add chicken, chorizo, and saffron.
14. Add the clams and shrimp, tucking them into the rice.
15. The shrimp will take about 8 minutes to cook.
16. Give the paella a good shake and let it simmer, without stirring, until the rice is al dente, for about 15 minutes.
17. During the last 5 minutes of cooking, when the rice is filling the pan, add the lobster tails.
18. When the paella is cooked and the rice looks fluffy and moist, turn the heat up for 40 seconds until you can smell the rice toast at the bottom, then it's perfect.
19. Remove from heat and rest for 5 minutes.
20. Garnish with peas, parsley and lemon wedges.

# Rice Pudding

## Ingredients:

2 cups water
1 cup Arborio rice
3 cups vanilla soy milk
1/4 cup sugar
1 pinch salt
1 cinnamon stick
1/2 tsp. vanilla extract
1/2 tsp. ground cinnamon, + more for dusting
1/4 tsp. ground nutmeg
2 tbsps. + 2 tsps. sweetened condensed milk

## Directions:

1. Preheat the oven to 375 degrees F.
2. Bring the water to a boil in a medium sized, heavy, ovenproof saucepan.
3. Add the rice, cover, and simmer for 20 minutes, until rice is nearly cooked.
4. In a large bowl, whisk the soymilk, sugar, and salt.
5. When the rice is cooked and still hot, add the soymilk mixture and cinnamon stick.
6. Cover, place in the oven and cook for 45 minutes.
7. Remove from the oven, uncover, and remove the cinnamon stick.
8. Stir in the vanilla, cinnamon and nutmeg.
9. Pudding will be slightly liquidy; the liquid will continue to absorb into the rice and thicken as the pudding cools.
10. Distribute among 8 bowls, drizzle each with 1 tsp. of the condensed milk.
11. Dust with cinnamon and nutmeg, if desired.
12. Serve warm or at room temperature.

# Rice with Fresh Herbs

## Ingredients:

1 1/2 cups long-grain white rice
1 tbsp. plus
1/2 tsp.
kosher salt, + extra if needed
2 tbsps. unsalted butter
1/4 cup finely chopped fresh herbs, such as basil, chives,
cilantro, mint, or tarragon

## Directions:

1. Bring a large pot of water to a boil over high heat.
2. Add the rice and 1 tbsp. of the salt and cook, stirring
   occasionally, until the rice is tender, 12 to 15 minutes.
3. Drain through a fine-mesh sieve and rinse under cold
   water to stop the cooking.
4. Shake the sieve to drain as much water as possible.
5. Melt the butter in a large nonstick skillet over medium
   heat.
6. Add the rice and the remaining 1/2 tsp. salt and stir
   with a heatproof rubber spatula to coat all the rice with
   the butter.
7. Once the rice is warmed through, about 3 minutes,
   transfer the rice to a serving bowl and add the herbs
   plus additional salt, if needed.
8. Stir with a fork to incorporate and fluff the rice and
   serve warm or at room temperature.

# Arroz Con Pollo

## Ingredients:

4 pieces chicken thighs, bone-in, skin on
4 chicken drumsticks
Salt and freshly ground black pepper
Paprika or smoked sweet paprika
2 tbsps. extra-virgin olive oil
1 tbsp. butter
1/2 cup 2-inch pieces vermicelli pasta
1 pinch saffron threads
2 cups chicken stock
5 oz. thick-cut speck, smoky ham or Serrano ham, diced
1 large onion or 2 medium onions, chopped
2 to 3 ribs celery, chopped
2 bell peppers, 1 red and 1 green
2 chile peppers, seeded and chopped
3 to 4 cloves garlic, chopped
1 bay leaf
1 large tomato, cored and chopped
1 cup long grain rice

## Directions:

1. Season the chicken liberally with salt, pepper, and paprika.
2. Add to a pre-heated large, shallow pot with 1 tbsp. extra-virgin olive oil. Once browned, remove the chicken to a plate and drain off the fat.
3. Add butter to the pot and melt. Brown the pasta 2 minutes or until golden, remove to plate and reserve.
4. Place the saffron and chicken stock in a small pot and warm it up to steep the saffron threads.
5. Once the pasta is browned and has been removed from the pot, add the remaining tbsp. extra-virgin olive oil, a turn of the pan, and brown the ham, about 2 minutes.
6. Add the onions, celery, bell peppers, hot peppers, garlic and bay leaf to the pan.

7. Cook 5 to 6 minutes to soften up a bit, then add the tomatoes, rice. Stir in the pasta and warm saffron stock.
8. Add the chicken and cover the pot, cook 18 minutes, until rice is tender.

# Taco Rice

## Ingredients:

2 tbsp. cooking oil
1 small onion
1 clove garlic
2 cups long grain white rice
1/2 tbsp. chili powder
1/2 tsp cumin
1/4 tsp oregano
3 cups water
1 tsp salt
2 green onions, sliced

## Directions:

1. Finely dice the onion and mince the garlic. Add the onion, garlic, and cooking oil to a medium sauce pot. Sauté the onion and garlic over medium heat until the onions are soft and transparent.
2. Add the uncooked rice, chili powder, cumin, and oregano to the pot.
3. Continue to stir and cook for about 2 minutes to toast the rice and spices. You should hear the rice making crackling noises.
4. Finally, add the water and salt, and give everything a brief stir.
5. Place a lid on the pot, turn the heat up to medium-high, and allow it to come to a boil.
6. As soon as it reaches a full boil, turn the heat down to low, or slightly above low, and let it simmer for 15 minutes.
7. After 15 minutes, turn the heat off and let it sit for 10 minutes without removing the lid.
8. After letting it rest for 10 minutes, fluff the rice with a fork.
9. Sprinkle sliced green onions over top just before serving.

# Chicken Fajita Rice Stuffed Peppers

## Ingredients:

3/4 cup dry brown rice (2 cups cooked)
5 medium red , yellow, orange or green bell peppers
1 medium yellow onion , chopped (1 1/2 cups)
2 cloves garlic , minced
2 tbsp. canola oil , divided
1 lb. chicken , diced into 3/4-inch pieces
1 tsp. chili powder
1 tsp. ground cumin
1/4 tsp paprika
Salt and freshly ground black pepper
1 (10 oz.) can tomatoes with green chiles
1 cup canned black beans , drained and rinsed
1 cup frozen corn
3 tbsp. fresh cilantro , plus more for garnish
1 tbsp. fresh lime juice
2/3 cup shredded monterey jack cheese
Sour cream
Mexican style hot sauce (such as Tapatio or Cholula)

## Directions:

1. Prepare brown rice according to directions listed on package.
2. Halfway through brown rice cooking, preheat oven to 375 degrees and begin making filling and boiling peppers.
3. Bring a large pot of water to a boil.
4. Cut peppers in half through length (top to bottom), seed and devein peppers, then boil 4 - 5 minutes (fully immersing them in the water), just until tender.
5. Drain well and align in baking pans, set aside.
6. Heat 1 tbsp. oil in a large and deep skillet over medium-high heat.

7. Add onions and sauté until golden about 5 minutes, then add garlic and sauté 30 seconds longer, transfer onion mixture to a plate.
8. Add remaining 1 tbsp. oil skillet, and add chicken, sprinkle with 1/2 tsp chili powder, 1/2 tsp cumin, the paprika and season with salt and pepper.
9. Cook, stirring occasionally, until cooked through, about 5 minutes.
10. Reduce heat to medium-low, add tomatoes, onion mixture, black beans, corn, cooked brown rice, remaining 1/2 tsp chili powder, 1/2 tsp cumin cumin, cilantro, lime juice and season with salt and pepper to taste.
11. Cook just until heated through.
12. Add a heaping 1/2 cup of the mixture to each pepper half (and slightly press as filling to fit).
13. Pour enough water into bottom of baking dishes to reach 1/8-inch in height (careful not to pour it in peppers).
14. Cover baking dishes with foil and bake 30 - 35 minutes, until peppers are soft.
15. Remove from oven, sprinkle tops evenly with cheese then return to oven to bake until cheese has melted, about 3 minutes longer.
16. Serve warm topped with more cilantro, sour cream and hot sauce if desired.

# Mediterranean Rice Bowl

## Ingredients:

2 cups brown or white basmati rice, uncooked
2 whole wheat pitas, or pita chips
2 pinches garlic powder
1 shallot
1 red pepper
1 English cucumber
8 cups salad greens
1/4 cup chopped fresh parsley
1/4 cup olive oil, plus additional for drizzling
1/2 tbsp. soy sauce
1/2 tsp. dried oregano
1/2 tsp. dried dill
1/2 tsp. dried thyme
3/4 cup prepared hummus
1/4 tsp. paprika
1 cup microgreens
1 lemon
Kosher salt

## Directions:

1. Prepare the rice in a rice maker or according to the package instructions.
2. If making homemade pita chips, preheat oven to 350F.
3. Lightly brush each pita with olive oil, then sprinkle with a few pinches kosher salt and a pinch of garlic powder.
4. Cut each pita into 8 wedges with a pizza cutter, then place the wedges on a baking sheet.
5. Bake until browned and crisp, about 15 minutes.
6. Thinly slice the shallot (into rings), red pepper, and cucumber.
7. Chop the parsley (optional). If necessary, wash and dry the salad greens.
8. In a small bowl, whisk together olive oil, soy sauce, oregano, dill, and thyme.

9. To serve, place the greens into bowls and top with the rice, then drizzle the rice with the olive oil mixture.
10. Add a dollop of hummus and sprinkle with paprika.
11. Top with shallot, red pepper, cucumber, microgreens and parsley (if using).
12. To serve, squeeze with lemon wedges, a drizzle of olive oil and a sprinkle of kosher salt.

# Rice with Parsley, Almonds, and Apricots

## Ingredients:

1 cup skin-on almonds
1 tbsp. olive oil
Kosher salt
1 cup basmati rice
1 3-inch strip lemon zest
1/3 cup chopped dried apricots
2 cups chopped parsley
1 tbsp. fresh lemon juice

## Directions:

1. Preheat oven to 300 degrees F.
2. Toss almonds with oil on a small rimmed baking sheet; season with salt.
3. Roast, tossing occasionally, until golden brown, 10–12 minutes.
4. Let cool, then chop.
5. Meanwhile, rinse rice in several changes of water until water runs clear.
6. Bring rice, lemon zest, and 1½ cups water to a boil in a small saucepan; season with salt.
7. Reduce heat, cover pan, and simmer until rice is tender, 18–20 minutes.
8. Remove from heat, uncover, and scatter apricots over rice.
9. Cover; let sit 10 minutes.
10. Fluff rice with a fork, then mix in almonds, parsley, and lemon juice.
11. Taste and season with more salt if needed.

# Pumpkin Pie Rice Pudding

## Ingredients:

1 cup short grain brown rice
2.5 cups almond milk, unsweetened
1/4 cup maple syrup
2 tsps. pumpkin pie spice
1/2 cup pumpkin puree

## Directions:

1. Place 1 cup brown rice, 2 cups almond milk, 1/4 cup maple syrup and 2 tsps. pumpkin pie spice in a medium-size pot and turn to high heat.
2. Bring to a boil.
3. Once boiling, turn to low and cover.
4. Let simmer for 30-35 minutes. At this point, there should still be some liquid left.
5. Add in 1/2 cup pumpkin puree and continue to let simmer for an additional 10-20 minutes or until the brown rice is cooked through and the consistency is thick.
6. Add in 1/2 cup more of almond milk and mix.
7. Serve hot.

# Broccoli Cheddar Brown Rice Skillet

## Ingredients:

2 tsps. canola oil, divided
1/2 small yellow onion, minced
Salt
Pepper
1 1/2 cups broccoli florets
1 cup cooked brown rice
2 tbsps. plain Greek yogurt
2 tbsps. nutritional yeast flakes
1/4 tsp. paprika
1 oz. cheddar, grated
Red pepper flakes

## Directions:

1. Heat oven to 400 degrees F.
2. In na oven-safe (preferably cast iron) skillet over medium heat, heat 1 tsp oil.
3. Add onion and cook, stirring occasionally, until it starts to soften, about 2 minutes.
4. Add garlic, salt, and pepper, and cook just until garlic is fragrant, about 1 minute more.
5. Add broccoli and 1 tbsp. water and reduce heat to medium low.
6. Cook, stirring, until broccoli is bright green but still very crunchy, about 2 minutes.
7. Add rice and cook, stirring, until just heated through.
8. Remove from heat.
9. In a bowl, stir together yogurt, yeast, paprika, curry powder, and remaining 1 tsp oil.
10. Pour over broccoli-rice mixture and toss to combine.
11. Spread into an even layer and top with cheese.
12. Bake until heated through and cheese starts to brown, about 15 minutes.
13. Cool slightly before serving.

14. Garnish with red pepper flakes, plus more black pepper, if desired.

# Parmesan Rice

## Ingredients:

4 tbsps. butter
1/2 medium sweet onion, chopped
3 cloves garlic, minced
1 1/2 cups uncooked long-grain rice
1 (14.5-oz.) can chicken broth
1 cup milk
1/2 tsp. salt
1/2 cup finely grated Parmesan cheese
1 tbsp. lemon juice

## Directions:

1. Melt butter in a medium pot.
2. Add onion and cook until softened.
3. Add garlic and rice.
4. Stir with a wooden spoon and cook 1 minute.
5. Add chicken broth and milk. Bring to a simmer.
6. Cover pot and reduce heat to low. Cook 20 minutes.
7. Remove from heat and stir in Parmesan cheese and lemon juice.

# Southwestern Rice

## Ingredients:

1 tbsp. olive oil
1 medium green pepper, diced
1 medium onion, chopped
2 garlic cloves, minced
1 cup uncooked long grain rice
1/2 tsp. ground cumin
1/8 tsp. ground turmeric
1 can (14-1/2 oz.) reduced-sodium chicken broth
2 cups frozen corn (about 10 oz.), thawed
1 can (15 oz.) black beans, rinsed and drained
1 can (10 oz.) diced tomatoes and green chilies, undrained

## Directions:

1. In a large nonstick skillet, heat oil over medium-high heat; sauté pepper and onion 3 minutes.
2. Add garlic; cook and stir 1 minute.
3. Stir in rice, spices and broth; bring to a boil. Reduce heat; simmer, covered, until rice is tender, about 15 minutes.
4. Stir in remaining ingredients.
5. Cook, covered, until heated through.

# Portuguese Rice

## Ingredients:

1/4 cup canola oil
1 yellow onion, finely chopped
3 garlic cloves, minced
3 cups long grain white rice, washed and drained
4 cups boiling water
1 bay leaf
2 medium tomatoes, chopped
1/2 tsp. salt

## Directions:

1. In a 4-quart pot, heat the oil over medium-high heat.
2. Add the onions and garlic and stir-fry until golden.
3. Add the rice and cook, stirring constantly, until slightly toasted and fragrant, 2 to 3 minutes.
4. Add the water, bay leaf, tomatoes and salt and bring to a boil.
5. Cover and reduce the heat so that the rice just simmers.
6. Cook undisturbed until tender, about 20 minutes.
7. Remove from the heat and let stand covered without stirring for 10 minutes.
8. Fluff with a fork, discard the bay leaf, and serve.

# Garlic Butter Rice

## Ingredients:

1/3 cup margarine
1/2 cup white or jasmine rice
2 chicken bouillon cubes
1 1/2 cups water or chicken broth
2 -3 tbsps. chopped garlic

## Directions:

1. Melt the butter or margarine in a 10" skillet over med-high heat.
2. Add the rice and stir.
3. Add the bouillon cube(s) and stir until softened or dissolved.
4. Watch closely so that the rice does not start to brown.
5. You might need to lower the heat if the rice starts to brown or appears to be cooking too fast.
6. Add the water and stir.
7. Cover with a lid and bring it to a boil.
8. Lower the heat to med to med-low and cook for 10 minutes or until rice is almost tender and a lot, but not all, of the water/butter mixture has been absorbed.
9. This comes out better if it is "slow cooked".
10. Add the garlic and stir.
11. Put the lid back on the skillet and continue cooking for 5 more minutes or until the rice is tender and all of the water has been absorbed.
12. There may still be some melted butter at the bottom of the skillet, but that is okay.
13. Stir well and turn the burner off.
14. Let the skillet sit on the burner until you are ready to serve the rice.

# Shrimp Fried Rice

## Ingredients:

1 tbsp. vegetable oil
2 cloves garlic, minced
2 carrots, peeled and finely chopped
1 green bell pepper, finely chopped
1 lb. shrimp, peeled and deveined
3 c. cooked white rice
1 c. frozen peas, defrosted
2 tbsp. soy sauce
2 tsp. sesame oil
1 large egg, whisked
Sriracha, for serving
2 tbsp. Sliced green onions

## Directions:

1. In a medium skillet over medium heat, heat oil.
2. Add garlic and stir for one minute. Add carrots and peppers and sauté, 3 minutes, then add shrimp and cook, 4 minutes, stirring occasionally.
3. Stir in rice and peas and season with soy sauce and sesame oil.
4. Sauté for 2 more minutes.
5. Push rice to one side of the skillet and add the egg.
6. Stir egg constantly until almost fully cooked, then fold into rice mixture.
7. Garnish with Sriracha and green onions and serve.

# Saffron Rice

## Ingredients:

2 cups uncooked long-grain rice
3/4 tsp. crushed saffron threads
4 tbsps. butter
6 whole cardamom seeds
4 whole cloves
3 cinnamon sticks
1 onion, chopped
3 cups boiling vegetable broth
1 tsp. salt

## Directions:

1. Cover rice with cold water and set aside to soak for 30 minutes.
2. Soak saffron threads in 2 tbsps. boiling water.
3. Melt butter in a large saucepan over medium heat.
4. Add cardamom, cloves and cinnamon and fry 2 minutes, stirring occasionally.
5. Stir in onion and sauté, stirring occasionally, until golden brown.
6. Stir in the rice, reduce heat to low and simmer for 5 minutes, stirring constantly.
7. Pour in the boiling broth and stir in the salt and saffron.
8. Cover and cook until rice is cooked and all liquid is absorbed, about 40 minutes.

# Baked Mushroom Rice

## Ingredients:

2 cups uncooked white rice
1 (10.75 oz.) can condensed cream of mushroom soup
1 cup vegetable broth
1/2 cup chopped onion
1/4 cup fresh chopped mushrooms
1 tsp. dried parsley
1 tsp. dried oregano
1/4 cup butter, melted
salt and pepper to taste

## Directions:

1. Preheat oven to 400 degrees F (200 degrees C).
2. In a large bowl, stir together the white rice, cream of mushroom soup, and vegetable broth.
3. Blend in the onion, mushrooms, parsley, oregano, melted butter, salt, and pepper.
4. Transfer to a 2 quart baking dish, and cover with a lid or aluminum foil.
5. Bake for 35 to 40 minutes in the preheated oven.
6. If the rice is looking dry before it is tender, then pour in a little water and continue cooking until rice is tender.

# Honey Rice

## Ingredients:

3 cups cooked rice
1/2 cup raisins
2 1/2 cups milk
1/2 cup honey
2 tbsps. butter
1 tsp. grated lemon rind
1 tbsp. lemon juice
1/8 tsp. ground cinnamon

## Directions:

1. Combine rice, raisins, milk, honey, and butter in a saucepan.
2. Bring the mixture to a boil, reduce the heat, and let it simmer for 15 minutes; stirring occasionally.
3. Stir in lemon rind and juice.
4. Serve the rice in bowls and garnish (optional) with cinnamon and slivered almonds.

# Orzo and Rice

## Ingredients:

2 tbsps. butter
1/2 cup uncooked orzo pasta
1/2 cup long-grain white rice
1 cube chicken bouillon
2 cups water

## Directions:

1. In a large heavy saucepan, melt butter over medium heat.
2. Add orzo and brown until golden.
3. Add rice, bouillon, and water; bring to a boil, cover and lower heat to medium-low.
4. Simmer for about 20 to 25 minutes or until all water is absorbed.
5. Serve and enjoy!

# Curried Rice

## Ingredients:

1 onion, finely diced
3 cloves garlic, finely diced
3 tbsps. olive oil
4 tsps. sweet curry
2 cups rice (dry)
2 tsps. salt
3-1/4 cups water

## Directions:

1. Cook onion and garlic in a 3-4 quart heavy saucepan over med-low heat until softened.
2. Add curry powder and rice and cook, stirring often, about 1 min.
3. Add water and salt and bring to a boil, uncovered, without stirring, until the surface of the rice is covered with steam holes and the grains on top appear dry (about 8 minutes).
4. Reduce heat to as low as possible, then cover with a tight fitting lid.
5. Cook another 15 minutes.
6. Remove pan from heat and let stand another five minutes before serving.

# Korean Curry Rice

## Ingredients:

8 oz. beef, pork or chicken
1 med. onion
1 tsp. minced garlic
1/2 tsp. grated ginger
2 med. potatoes
1 large carrot
4 caps white mushrooms
1/2 green bell pepper
1/2 pkg. instant curry roux
4 cups water (or chicken broth)
4 servings of cooked rice

## Directions:

1. Cut the meat into small bite size pieces.
2. Lightly sprinkle with salt and pepper.
3. Dice the onion, and cut the other vegetables into bite size chunks.
4. Heat a large pot with a tbsp. of oil.
5. Add the onion, and stir-fry until it turns translucent and light brown.
6. Add the meat, garlic and ginger, and cook until the meat is no longer pink.
7. Add the remaining vegetables and stir fry until potatoes turn translucent and partially cooked.
8. Pour the water (or chicken broth) into the pot.
9. Bring it to a boil, and continue to boil for about 10 minutes until the meat becomes tender.
10. Break up the curry roux into small cubes. Drop them in, and stir well to dissolve.
11. Reduce the heat to medium low, and gently boil until the sauce is thickened. Serve over steamed rice. Add more water if too thick.

# Ginger Curry Rice

## Ingredients:

2 cups uncooked rice
2 cups chicken stock, salt added
1/2 cup fresh ginger, thinly sliced
5 clove of garlic, crushed
1 pinch black pepper
2 tbsp. curry powder

## Directions:

1. In a bowl, mix curry powder and chicken stock until well mix.
2. In a medium size cooking pot, add chicken stock mixture, black pepper, ginger, and garlic, bring to boil. When done set to cool.
3. In a rice cooking pot, washed and rinse the rice.
4. When done rinsing, add and measure the stock into rice for even amount before cooking.
5. Ginger and garlic may added into your rice for better taste.
6. When cooked, place rice onto serving plate, top with spring onion.
7. Serve with chicken babaque or roasted chicken with a side of cucumber.
8. Thai sweet chili sauce can be serve with your chicken.

# Chicken Curry And Rice

## Ingredients:

3 1/2 tbsps. oil, divided
2 1/2 cups boneless skinless chicken breasts
4 tsps. mild curry powder divided
Salt and pepper
1 cup red pepper chopped
1 cup snap peas tops removed
2 tsps. minced garlic
1 tbsp. fresh ginger grated
1 tbsp. cornstarch
1 1/2 tsps. white sugar
3 cups chicken broth divided
1 cup white rice
1/3 cup sour cream
Finely chopped cilantro
Fresh naan bread

## Directions:

1. Slice the chicken into small and thin chunks.
2. Massage the chunks evenly with 2 tsps. curry powder and salt and pepper.
3. In a large pot add 2 tbsps. oil over medium heat.
4. Add the chicken chunks and stir around until no longer pink on the outside, about 5 minutes.
5. Do not cook them all the way through.
6. Transfer the partially cooked chicken to a plate.
7. In the same pot, add in the remaining 1 and 1/2 tbsps. oil.
8. Stir in the garlic and ginger and stir until fragrant over low heat.
9. Add in the red pepper and green snap peas.
10. Stir until slightly tender, about 4-5 minutes and then add the remaining 2 tsps. curry powder in.
11. Whisk the cornstarch into 2 cups of the chicken broth until the cornstarch is dissolved and then pour the mixture on top of the vegetables.

12. Allow the mixture to come to a boil and then reduce the heat to allow it to slightly thicken.
13. Add the chicken back in along with the rice, sugar, and remaining 1 cup of chicken broth.
14. Bring to a boil once more and then reduce the heat to low and cover with a lid.
15. Allow to cook until the rice is cooked through and tender and the chicken and veggies are all cooked through.
16. Season with salt and pepper and any additional curry powder if desired.
17. Stir in the Greek yogurt or sour cream and serve immediately.
18. Add chopped cilantro and serve with fresh naan if desired,

# Panang Chicken Curry and Red Bean Rice

## Curry Ingredients:

6 cups full-fat coconut milk, with 3 tbsp. of the cream separated out
4 tbsp. Panang curry paste
2 kaffir lime leaves, cut into a fine chiffonade
1/2 cup thinly sliced brown onion
1/2 cup roughly chopped, Thai sweet basil
1 1/2 lb. chicken breast, sliced into 1/4 in. thick tiles
1 cup canned sliced bamboo shoots
1/2 cup sliced red bell pepper
2 tsp fish sauce
1/2 tbsp. tamarind paste
1 tsp sugar

## Korean Red Bean Mixed Rice Ingredients:

1 cup adzuki beans, dry
2 cups plus 1 ¼ cup water, divided
1 cup short-grain rice

## Panang Chicken Curry Directions:

1. In a medium saucepan, heat the 3 tbsps. of the thick coconut cream on high for about 1 minute.
2. When the cream starts to sizzle, stir the curry paste into the cream like building a roux.
3. Add the lime leaves. Stir-fry the paste for about 1 minute, until the paste starts to thicken, dry out and become fragrant.
4. If the curry starts to sputter, add a small amount of coconut milk to keep the paste moving.
5. Cook the paste until it has the consistency of peanut butter.
6. Stir the onion, basil and remaining coconut milk into the curry paste.

7. Heat until you reach a full rolling boil. Allow the curry to boil for about 10 to 20 minutes or until it reduces by about one-fourth or coats the back of a wooden spoon.
8. Reduce the heat to a simmer.
9. Add the chicken, bamboo shoots, red bell pepper, fish sauce, tamarind and sugar.
10. Let this simmer for about 10 minutes, or until the chicken is cooked through.
11. Serve hot over cooked rice.

## Korean Red Bean Mixed Rice Directions:

1. Soak beans in 2 cups of water for about 4 hours to overnight.
2. Drain the beans with a fine mesh strainer but reserve 1 cup of the soaking water.
3. Transfer the beans and rice to a 1-quart saucepan or rice cooker and add 1 1/4 cup if water, plus the reserved 1 cup of soaking water.
4. Bring your heat to high.
5. As soon as the water reaches a boil, give everything a good stir, reduce to a low simmer and cover the pot.
6. After 20 minutes, turn off the burner, remove the pot from the heat and let it sit for at least 15 minutes before fluffing with a fork and serving.

# Cilantro Rice

## Ingredients:

3 1/2 cups packed cilantro leaves
3 med. garlic cloves
1 med. serrano chile, halved lengthwise and seeded
3 1/3 cups chicken broth
1 tbsp. vegetable oil
1/2 cup minced yellow onion
2 cups long-grain white rice
1 tbsp. kosher salt

## Directions:

1. Combine cilantro, garlic, chile, and 2 cups broth in a blender and process until smooth; set aside.
2. Heat oil in a large frying pan over medium-high heat.
3. When it shimmers, add onion and cook until softened, about 2 minutes.
4. Add rice and salt stir to coat in oil and cook until rice becomes opaque, about 2 minutes.
5. Carefully pour the cilantro mixture and the remaining 1 1/3 cups broth into the rice and stir to combine.
6. Bring mixture to a boil then reduce heat to low so rice is at a simmer.
7. Cover and cook until rice is tender, about 15 minutes.
8. Turn off heat and let rice rest covered for 5 minutes.
9. Fluff with fork and serve.

# Baked Brown Rice

## Ingredients:

1 1/2 cups brown rice, medium or short grain
2 1/2 cups water
1 tbsp. unsalted butter
1 tsp. kosher salt

## Directions:

1. Preheat the oven to 375 degrees F.
2. Place the rice into an 8-inch square glass baking dish.
3. Bring the water, butter, and salt just to a boil in a kettle or covered saucepan.
4. Once the water boils, pour it over the rice, stir to combine, and cover the dish tightly with heavy-duty aluminum foil.
5. Bake on the middle rack of the oven for 1 hour.
6. After 1 hour, remove cover and fluff the rice with a fork.

# Cranberry and Orange Wild Rice

## Ingredients:

1/2 cup dried cranberries
1 1/4 cups water
1 cup fresh orange juice
1 tbsp. unsalted butter
1 (8-oz.) pkg. long-grain and wild rice
1 orange, zested
1/2 cup sliced almonds

## Directions:

1. Put cranberries in a medium bowl and pour in enough hot tap water to cover. Set aside while you make the rice.
2. In a medium pot over medium-high heat, add the water, orange juice, and butter, and bring to a boil. Stir in the rice, and the included contents of the seasoning packet, and return to a boil.
3. Turn the heat to low, cover, and cook until the rice is tender, about 20 to 25 minutes.
4. Drain the cranberries and add them to the rice along with the orange zest, and almonds. Gently stir them in, fluffing the rice.
5. Transfer the rice to a serving bowl, cover and keep warm until ready to serve.

# Broccoli Wild Rice Casserole

## Ingredients:

2 cups uncooked wild rice
8 cups chicken broth, plus more if needed
3 heads broccoli, cut into small florets
8 tbsps. (1 stick) butter
1 lb. white button or cremini mushrooms, finely chopped
1 med. onion, finely diced
2 carrots, peeled and finely diced
2 stalks celery, finely diced
1/4 cup all-purpose flour
1/2 cup heavy cream
1 tsp. salt, or more to taste
1 tsp. black pepper, or more to taste
1 cup panko breadcrumbs
2 tbsps. minced fresh parsley

## Directions:

1. Add the wild rice to a medium saucepan with 5 cups of the chicken broth.
2. Bring to a boil over medium-high heat, then reduce the heat to low and cover the pan.
3. Cook until the rice has just started to break open and is slightly tender, 35 to 40 minutes. Set aside.
4. Meanwhile, bring a pot of water to a boil and prepare an ice water bath.
5. Blanch the broccoli by throwing the florets into the boiling water until bright green and still slightly crisp, 1 1/2 to 2 minutes.
6. Immediately drain the broccoli and plunge it into the bowl of ice water to stop the cooking process.
7. Remove it from the ice water and set aside.

8. Heat a large pot over medium-high heat, then melt 6 tbsps. of the butter. Add the mushrooms and onions and cook, stirring occasionally, until the liquid begins to evaporate, 3 to 4 minutes.
9. Add the carrots and celery and cook until the vegetables are soft and the mixture begins to turn darker in color, 3 to 4 minutes.
10. Sprinkle the flour on the vegetables, stir to incorporate it and cook for about a minute.
11. Pour in the remaining 3 cups of broth and stir to combine.
12. Bring the mixture to a gentle boil and allow it to thicken, about 3 minutes. Pour in the heavy cream, stirring to combine.
13. Let the mixture cook until it thickens. Add the salt and pepper, then taste and adjust the seasonings as needed.
14. Preheat the oven to 375 degrees F.
15. Mix together the cooked rice and broccoli and tip into a 2-quart baking dish.
16. Using a ladle, scoop out the vegetable/broth mixture and spoon it evenly all over the top, totally covering the surface with the vegetables.
17. Melt the remaining 2 tbsps. butter, then pour it into a separate bowl with the panko breadcrumbs.
18. Toss the mixture together to coat the breadcrumbs in butter, then sprinkle the breadcrumbs all over the top of the casserole.
19. Cover with foil and bake the casserole for 20 minutes, then remove the foil and continue baking until golden brown on top, another 15 minutes.
20. Sprinkle on the parsley after you remove it from the oven.

# Risotto

## Ingredients:

1 1/2 cups arborio rice
1 qt. chicken stock
1/2 cup vermouth or another dry white wine
1 med. shallot or 1/2 small onion, chopped
3 tbsp. whole butter, divided
1 tbsp. vegetable oil
1/4 cup grated Parmesan cheese
1 tbsp. chopped Italian parsley
Kosher salt, to taste

## Directions:

1. Heat the stock to a simmer in a medium saucepan, then lower the heat so that the stock just stays hot.
2. In a large, heavy-bottomed saucepan, heat the oil and 1 tbsp. of the butter over medium heat.
3. When the butter has melted, add the chopped shallot or onion. Sauté for 2–3 minutes or until slightly translucent.
4. Add the rice to the pot and stir it briskly with a wooden spoon so that the grains are coated with the oil and melted butter.
5. Sauté for another minute or so, until there is a slightly nutty aroma.
6. But don't let the rice turn brown.
7. Add the wine and cook while stirring, until the liquid is fully absorbed.
8. Add a ladle of hot chicken stock to the rice and stir until the liquid is fully absorbed. When the rice appears almost dry, add another ladle of stock and repeat the process.
9. It's important to stir constantly, especially while the hot stock gets absorbed, to prevent scorching, and add the next ladle as soon as the rice is almost dry.
10. Continue adding ladles of hot stock and stirring the rice while the liquid is absorbed.

11. As it cooks, you'll see that the rice will take on a creamy consistency as it begins to release its natural starches.
12. After 20–30 minutes or until the grains are tender but still firm to the bite, without being crunchy.
13. If you run out of stock and the risotto still isn't done, you can finish the cooking using hot water.
14. Just add the water as you did with the stock, a ladle at a time, stirring while it's absorbed.
15. Stir in the remaining 2 tbsp. butter, the Parmesan cheese, and the parsley, and season to taste with Kosher salt.

# Mushroom Risotto

## Ingredients:

6 cups chicken broth, divided
3 tbsps. olive oil, divided
1 lb. portobello mushrooms, thinly sliced
1 lb. white mushrooms, thinly sliced
2 shallots, diced
1 1/2 cups Arborio rice
1/2 cup dry white wine
Sea salt to taste
Freshly ground black pepper to taste
3 tbsps. finely chopped chives
4 tbsps. butter
1/3 cup freshly grated Parmesan cheese

## Directions:

1. In a saucepan, warm the broth over low heat.
2. Warm 2 tbsps. olive oil in a large saucepan over medium-high heat.
3. Stir in the mushrooms, and cook until soft, about 3 minutes.
4. Remove mushrooms and their liquid, and set aside.
5. Add 1 tbsp. olive oil to skillet, and stir in the shallots.
6. Cook 1 minute. Add rice, stirring to coat with oil, about 2 minutes.
7. When the rice has taken on a pale, golden color, pour in wine, stirring constantly until the wine is fully absorbed.
8. Add 1/2 cup broth to the rice, and stir until the broth is absorbed.
9. Continue adding broth 1/2 cup at a time, stirring continuously, until the liquid is absorbed and the rice is al dente, about 15 to 20 minutes.
10. Remove from heat, and stir in mushrooms with their liquid, butter, chives, and parmesan. Season with salt and pepper to taste.

# Risotto alla Milanese

## Ingredients:

14 oz. risotto rice
4 cups chicken stock, plus more as needed
3 tbsps. extra-virgin olive oil
1 small yellow onion, minced
1 cup dry white wine
2 pinches saffron
Kosher salt
2 tbsps. unsalted butter
1 1/2 oz. freshly grated Parmigiano-Reggiano cheese, + more for serving
1/2 cup heavy cream, whipped to stiff peaks

## Directions:

1. Combine rice and stock in a large bowl. Agitate rice with fingers or a whisk to release starch.
2. Strain through a fine-mesh strainer set over a 2-quart liquid cup measure or large bowl. Allow to drain well, shaking rice of excess liquid.
3. Heat oil in a heavy 12-inch sauté pan over medium-high heat until shimmering.
4. Add rice and cook, stirring and tossing frequently, until all liquid has evaporated and rice sizzles and takes on a nutty aroma, about 5 minutes.
5. Add onion and continue to cook, stirring frequently, until aromatic, about 1 minute. Add wine and cook, stirring occasionally, until the pan is nearly dry, about 3 minutes.
6. Give reserved stock a good stir and pour all but 1 cup over rice.
7. Add saffron and a large pinch of salt, increase heat to high, and bring to a simmer.
8. Stir rice once, making sure no stray grains are clinging to side of pan above the liquid.
9. Cover and reduce heat to lowest possible setting.
10. Cook rice for 10 minutes undisturbed.

11. Stir once, shake pan gently to redistribute rice, cover, and continue cooking until liquid is mostly absorbed and rice is tender with just a faint bite, about 5 minutes longer.
12. Remove lid. Stir remaining 1 cup of stock to distribute starch, then stir into rice.
13. Increase heat to high, add butter, and cook, stirring and shaking rice constantly until butter has melted and rice is thick and creamy.
14. Add more stock or water as necessary if risotto becomes too dry.
15. Off heat, add cheese and stir rapidly to thoroughly incorporate.
16. Fold in heavy cream, if using.
17. Season with salt. Serve immediately on hot plates, passing more cheese at the table.

# Green Risotto with Mushrooms

## Ingredients:

1/2 cup loosely packed fresh parsley leaves
1/4 cup loosely packed fresh tarragon leaves
6 cups vegetable stock or water, divided
2 cups loosely packed fresh spinach leaves
4 scallions, whites finely chopped, greens reserved separately
4 tbsps. extra-virgin olive oil
2 med. cloves garlic, minced
1 1/2 cups risotto-style rice
2 tbsps. canola or vegetable oil
8 oz. mixed wild mushrooms, cleaned and sliced
1 small shallot, minced
1 tsp. juice and 1 tsp. grated zest from 1 lemon
1 tsp. soy sauce
Kosher salt
Freshly ground black pepper

## Directions:

1. Finely chop 1 tbsp. parsley leaves and 1 tbsp. tarragon leaves.
2. Cover with a damp paper towel and refrigerate until ready to use.
3. Prepare a large ice bath.
4. In a medium saucepan, bring stock to a boil over high heat.
5. Add spinach, remaining whole parsley and tarragon leaves, and scallion greens.
6. Press down with a wire mesh spider to submerge.
7. Cook for 30 seconds, then transfer to ice bath and chill completely.
8. Remove stock from heat.

9. Transfer blanched greens to the jar of a blender and add 1/2 cup broth. Blend on high speed until completely smooth, about 30 seconds. Transfer to a small bowl and set aside.
10. Heat oil in a heavy 12-inch skillet over medium-high heat until foaming subsides.
11. Add rice and cook, stirring and tossing frequently until all liquid is evaporated, fat is bubbling, and rice has begun to take on a pale golden blond color and nutty aroma, about 3 minutes.
12. Add garlic and scallion whites and continue to cook, stirring frequently until aromatic, about 1 minute.
13. Add all but 1 1/2 cups of broth to skillet.
14. Stir rice once, cover, and reduce heat to lowest possible setting.
15. Cook rice for ten minutes undisturbed.
16. Stir once, shake pan gently to redistribute rice, cover, and continue cooking until liquid is mostly absorbed and rice is tender with just a faint bite, about 10 minutes longer.
17. Meanwhile, heat canola or vegetable oil in a 10-inch skillet over medium-high heat until shimmering.
18. Add mushrooms and cook, tossing occasionally, until well browned, about 5 minutes.
19. Add shallot and cook, stirring constantly, until aromatic, about 30 seconds.
20. Carefully add 1/4 cup broth, lemon juice, and soy sauce.
21. Remove from heat, toss to combine, season to taste with salt and pepper, and set aside.
22. Remove lid from risotto, add remaining broth, Increase heat to high and cook, stirring and shaking rice constantly until thick and creamy.
23. Off heat, stir in green puree, lemon zest, chopped parsley, and chopped tarragon.
24. Season to taste with salt and pepper. Serve immediately on hot plates, topping with mushrooms and their pan juices.

# Buffalo Ranch Chicken and Rice

## Ingredients:

2 lbs. boneless, skinless chicken breasts
4 cups chicken broth
1/3 cup Buffalo wing sauce
3 tbsps. ranch dressing mix, (1 oz. packet)
2 cups white rice
1/2 cup shredded Mexican blend cheese
Sliced green onions, optional

## Directions:

1. Dice uncooked chicken into bite-sized pieces.
2. Spray a dutch oven or other wide, deep pot with cooking spray.
3. Heat over medium-high heat. Add chicken, and sauté for a few minutes just to cook meat on outside.
4. Pour in broth, wing sauce, and ranch mix. Bring to a low boil.
5. Stir in uncooked rice.
6. Turn down heat to a low simmer.
7. Cover and cook 20 minutes.
8. Remove cover, and stir.
9. Rice should be cooked and liquid absorbed at this point. If not, simmer a few more minutes until rice is cooked completely.
10. Stir in cheese.
11. Sprinkle with additional cheese and sliced green onions if desired.

# Sriracha Fried Rice

## Ingredients:

2 tbsps. peanut or vegetable oil
1 clove garlic, minced
1 tsp. minced ginger
2 scallions, white and green parts separated and thinly sliced
5 or 6 fresh shiitake mushrooms, stems removed and caps finely chopped
1/2 cup frozen peas
3 cups cold leftover rice
3 tbsps. Sriracha
3 tbsp. soy sauce
2 tsps. sesame oil
Freshly ground black or white pepper to taste

## Directions:

1. Break up the cold cooked rice into smaller clumps.
2. Heat a wok or large skillet over medium-high heat until a bead of water sizzles and evaporates on contact.
3. Add the oil and swirl to coat the base.
4. Add the garlic, ginger, and scallion whites and cook for about 30 seconds, until just aromatic.
5. And the mushrooms and stir-fry for about 1 minute.
6. Toss in the rice and break up any remaining clumps with a spatula.
7. Add the peas.
8. Continue to stir-fry until the rice starts to turn golden, about 2 minutes.
9. Stir in the Sriracha, soy sauce, and sesame oil.
10. Add pepper to taste.
11. Optional: In a separate pan, fry an egg to top off the fried rice.
12. Sprinkle a little salt and pepper on the egg if you'd like.
13. Transfer the rice to bowls, sprinkle the scallion greens on top, and serve.

# Cajun Fried Rice

## Ingredients:

1 1⁄2 tbsps. soy sauce
2 tsps. toasted sesame oil, divided
2 garlic cloves, minced
2 tsps. minced gingerroot
3 tsps. Tabasco sauce
1⁄2 lb peeled crayfish tails or 1⁄2 lb shrimp
3 eggs
1 1⁄4 tsps. salt, divided
3 tbsps. peanut oil, divided
1 small onion, quartered and thinly sliced
3 cups cold cooked rice
1 1⁄2 cups bean sprouts
3⁄4 cup frozen green pea
Pepper

## Directions:

1. In small bowl combine soy sauce, 1 tsp sesame oil, garlic, ginger, and 2 tsp Tabasco.
2. Mix well; stir in crawfish and set aside.
3. In another bowl beat eggs with 1/4 tsp salt, remaining sesame oil, and Tabasco.
4. Heat wok or large skillet until hot.
5. Add 1 tbsp. oil and crawfish mixture.
6. Stir-fry 3-4 minutes or until crawfish are done.
7. Remove from wok and set aside.
8. Add another tbsp.. oil to wok; add onion.
9. Stir-fry 1-2 minutes and remove.
10. Heat remaining 1 tbsp. oil in wok.
11. Add egg mixture.
12. Stir-fry 1 minute or until done.
13. Add cold rice and stir-fry 3-4 minutes.
14. Add everything to wok and cook 2 minutes longer.

# Minnesota Wild Rice Soup

## Ingredients:

1 lb. lean ground beef
1/2 tsp. salt
1 tbsp. Italian seasoning
1 cup raw wild rice
1/2 tsp. black pepper
4 ribs celery, sliced
2 lg. onions, sliced
1 cup water
3 drops Tabasco sauce
2 tsp. beef bouillon
3 (10 oz.) cans cream of mushroom soup
2 soup cans water

## Directions:

1. In a large 4 quart heavy kettle, brown the beef with the salt and Italian seasoning, crumbling the meat as it cooks.
2. Add the wild rice, 1 cup water, Tabasco sauce, bouillon granules, pepper, celery and onion.
3. Simmer, covered, for about 30 minutes.
4. Stir in the soup and cans of water.
5. Cover and simmer another 30 minutes.

# Ham, Shrimp, Rice Dish

## Ingredients:

2 cup cooked ham
4 cup cooked rice
1 whole onion
3 cloves garlic
2 to 3 tomatoes
2 tbsp. fresh basil
1 green pepper
1 stick butter
1/2 lbs. of shrimp
1 lemon
2 bay leaves

## Directions:

1. Sauté onions, garlic and peppers in 1/2 stick of butter.
2. Stir in tomatoes.
3. Add shrimp and 1/2 of butter.
4. Season with bay leaves, basil, juice of 1 lemon, and dash of red pepper.
5. Add rice.
6. Toss.
7. Reduce heat to low and simmer for 10 minutes.

# Hearty Tomato Rice Soup

## Ingredients:

2 tbsps. butter
1 lb. hamburger
1 cup onion, chopped
1/2 cup celery, chopped
1 large can tomatoes
2 1/2 cup water
2 beef bouillon cubes
1/3 cup dry rice
salt and pepper to taste
1 tsp. fresh basil or half tsp. dried
2 tbsps. fresh parsley, chopped
3 garlic cloves, minced or 1/2 tsp. garlic powder

## Directions:

1. Sauté hamburger and onion in butter; add celery.
2. Break up hamburger into small pieces.
3. Combine with remaining ingredients.
4. Cook over low heat 30 minutes or until rice is tender.

# Hamburger-Rice Skillet

## Ingredients:

1 lb. ground beef or 1 lb. ground pork
1 med. onion, sliced and separated into rings
1 med. green pepper, coarsely chopped
1 garlic clove, minced
1 cup medium grain rice
1 (16 oz.) can diced tomatoes
1 (8 oz.) can tomato sauce
1 tsp. Worcestershire sauce
1/2 tsp. dried basil
1 1/2 cups water
1 tsp. salt
1/2 cup cheese, shredded

## Directions:

1. In a skillet coated with spray oil, brown ground beef, onion, green pepper, and garlic until meat is browned.
2. Drain off fat.
3. Add rice; cook stirring constantly, for 2 minutes.
4. Add remaining ingredients (except cheese).
5. Bring to a boil, reduce heat.
6. Cover and simmer for 25 to 30 minutes or until rice is tender, stirring occasionally.
7. Remove cover, sprinkle with cheese, if desired.

# Cheesy Burger, Rice and Broccoli Skillet

## Ingredients:

1 lb. lean ground beef
1 (10 3/4-oz.) can condensed cream of chicken soup
1 (8-oz.) can tomato sauce
2 tsps. Worcestershire sauce
4 to 5 drops hot pepper sauce
1 cup uncooked regular long-grain white rice
2 cups water
4 cups frozen broccoli florets
4 oz. (1 cup) shredded sharp Cheddar cheese

## Directions:

1. Brown ground beef in 12-inch nonstick skillet over medium-high heat until thoroughly cooked, stirring frequently. Drain.
2. Add soup, tomato sauce, Worcestershire sauce and hot pepper sauce; mix well.
3. Stir in rice and water. Bring mixture to a boil.
4. Reduce heat to low; cover and simmer 15 to 20 minutes or until rice is tender and liquid is absorbed, stirring once or twice.
5. Meanwhile, cook broccoli to desired doneness as directed on package. Drain; set aside.
6. Stir cooked broccoli into ground beef mixture; mix well.
7. Sprinkle with cheese.
8. Cover; cook an additional 5 minutes or until cheese is melted.

# Beef Taco Rice Skillet

## Ingredients:

1 lb. ground beef
1 envelope (1 oz.) taco seasoning mix
1 1/2 cups water
1 cup chunky salsa
1 cup frozen whole kernel corn
1 1/2 cups uncooked instant rice
3/4 cup shredded taco-seasoned cheese
1 cup shredded lettuce
1 med. tomato, chopped (3/4 cup)
Sour cream, if desired

## Directions:

1. In 10-inch skillet, cook beef over medium heat 8 to 10 minutes, stirring occasionally, until brown; drain.
2. Stir in taco seasoning mix, water, salsa and corn.
3. Heat to boiling; stir in rice. Boil 1 minute; remove from heat. Cover; let stand 8 minutes.
4. Fluff rice mixture with fork; sprinkle with cheese.
5. Cover; let stand 1 to 2 minutes or until cheese is melted.
6. Sprinkle lettuce around edge of skillet; sprinkle tomato in circle next to lettuce. Serve with sour cream.

# Greek Lemon Pilaf

## Ingredients:

2 tbsps. butter or 2 tbsps. margarine
1/2 cup chopped onion
1 cup long grain rice
2 tbsps. orzo pasta
2 cups chicken broth
1/4 cup lemon juice
2 tbsps. chopped parsley

## Directions:

1. In a heavy saucepan, sauté onion in butter until tender.
2. Add rice and orzo and cook, stirring, for 2 minutes.
3. Add chicken broth and lemon juice and bring to a boil.
4. Reduce heat, cover, and simmer for 20 minutes or until rice is tender and liquid has been absorbed.
5. Fluff pilaf up with fork and stir in chopped parsley.

# Indian Rice Pilaf

## Ingredients:

1/4 cup water
1 (14.5 oz.) can chicken broth
1 cup long grain rice
1 tsp. curry powder
1/2 tsp. garlic powder
1/4 tsp. ground cinnamon
1/8 tsp. paprika
2 pinches ground cloves
1 sm. onion, coarsely chopped

## Directions:

1. Bring water and chicken broth to a boil.
2. Combine rice, curry powder, garlic powder, cinnamon, paprika, and cloves in a bowl; stir to mix.
3. Add spiced rice and onion to the boiling broth.
4. Cover and cook until rice is tender, 20 to 25 minutes.

# Sun Dried Tomato Risotto

## Ingredients:

1 oz. sun-dried tomatoes (not packed in oil, about 10)
1 cup water
2 1/2 cups chicken broth
1 cup finely chopped onion
1 garlic clove, minced
4 tbsps. olive oil
1 cup Arborio rice
1/4 cup freshly grated Parmesan
Finely chopped fresh parsley leaves for sprinkling

## Directions:

1. In a small saucepan simmer the tomatoes in the water for 1 minute, drain them, reserving the liquid, and chop them.
2. In a saucepan combine the reserved cooking liquid and the broth, bring the liquid to a simmer, and keep it at a bare simmer.
3. In a large saucepan cook the onion and the garlic in the oil over moderately low heat, stirring, until they are softened, add the rice, stirring until each grain is coated with oil, and stir in the tomatoes.
4. Add 1/2 cup of the simmering liquid and cook the mixture over moderate heat, stirring constantly, until the liquid is absorbed.
5. Continue adding the liquid, 1/2 cup at a time, stirring constantly and letting each portion be absorbed before adding the next, until the rice is tender but still al dente, about 17 minutes
6. Stir in the Parmesan and salt and pepper to taste and sprinkle the risotto with the parsley.

# Feta Rice Pilaf

## Ingredients:

2 tbsps. butter
1/2 cup orzo pasta
1/2 cup diced onion
2 cloves garlic, minced
1/2 cup white rice
2 cups chicken broth
1 cup chopped spinach
1/2 cup chopped Bulgarian feta cheese

## Directions:

1. Melt butter in a skillet over medium-low heat; cook and stir orzo in the melted butter until golden brown, 3 to 5 minutes.
2. Stir onion into orzo and cook until translucent, 5 to 10 minutes.
3. Cook and stir garlic into orzo-onion mixture until fragrant, about 1 minute.
4. Mix rice and chicken broth into orzo-onion mixture; bring to a boil.
5. Reduce heat to medium-low, cover skillet, and simmer until rice is tender and liquid is absorbed, 20 to 25 minutes.
6. Remove from heat and stir in spinach and feta. Cover and let stand until spinach is wilted and feta is melted, about 5 minutes.
7. Fluff with a fork.

# Pork Fried Rice Recipe

## Ingredients:

3 tbsps. soy sauce
5 tsps. rice vinegar
1 tbsp. sesame oil
1/4 tsp. sugar
1/4 cup solid vegetable shortening
3/4 pound Chinese barbecued pork, cut into small cubes 1/3 inch thick
1/2 cup frozen peas, thawed
2 large shiitake mushrooms, stems discarded and caps thinly sliced
1 carrot, cut into 1/3-inch dice
1 head baby bok choy, halved lengthwise and thinly sliced crosswise
4 large eggs, lightly beaten
6 cups cold cooked Japanese short-grain rice
2 scallions, thinly sliced
1 pinch of freshly ground pepper
Kosher salt
1/4 cup pickled ginger

## Directions:

1. In a small bowl, stir the soy sauce with the rice vinegar, sesame oil and sugar.
2. Heat a very large skillet. Add the shortening and let melt.
3. Add the diced pork and stir-fry over high heat for 1 minute.
4. Add the peas, shiitakes, carrot and bok choy and stir-fry until tender.
5. Add the eggs and scramble just until set.
6. Stir in the cooked rice, scallions, soy sauce mixture and pepper and stir-fry until the rice is hot.
7. Remove from the heat and season with salt.
8. Spoon the fried rice into bowls, top with the sliced pork and pickled ginger and serve.

# Ranch Chicken and Rice

## Ingredients:

1 packet ranch salad dressing and seasoning mix
1 1/2 pounds boneless, skinless chicken breast, cut into 1-inch pieces
1 tbsp. canola oil
1 yellow onion
1 green bell pepper, cored, seeded and chopped
15.5 oz. can black beans, rinsed
28 oz. can fire roasted diced tomatoes
1½ cups instant rice
1½ cups chicken stock
1 small jalapeño
Freshly chopped cilantro

## Directions:

1. In a bowl, toss the chicken with half of the seasoning mix until well coated.
2. In a large skillet, heat the oil over medium high heat.
3. Add the chicken to the skillet and cook on all sides for 2 to 3 minutes or just until browned and cooked through (165°F).
4. Add the onion, bell pepper and cook stirring for another 2 minutes.
5. Add the beans, tomatoes and rice.
6. In a small bowl, stir the remaining seasoning mix into the stock until well blended. Pour the stock into the skillet and bring to a simmer.
7. Reduce the heat and cook for 5 minutes or until all of the stock has been absorbed.
8. Sprinkle the jalapeño on top and garnish with cilantro.
9. Refrigerate or discard leftovers within two hours of preparation.

# About the Author

Laura Sommers is **The Recipe Lady!**

She is a loving wife and mother who lives on a small farm in Baltimore County, Maryland and has a passion for all things domestic especially when it comes to saving money. She has a profitable eBay business and is a couponing addict. Follow her tips and tricks to learn how to make delicious meals on a budget, save money or to learn the latest life hack!

Visit her Amazon Author Page to see her latest books:

## amazon.com/author/laurasommers

Visit the Recipe Lady's blog for even more great recipes:

## http://the-recipe-lady.blogspot.com/

Follow the Recipe Lady on **Pinterest**:

## http://pinterest.com/therecipelady1

# Other Books by Laura Sommers

- **Gluten Free Cauliflower Recipes**
- **Spinach Recipes**
- **Fruit Smoothie Recipes**
- **Eggplant Recipes**
- **Zucchini Recipes**
- **Broccoli Recipes**

May all of your meals be a banquet
with good friends and good food.

Printed in Great Britain
by Amazon

46054010R00051